THE ADVENTURES OF
PARK RANGER
BROCK CLIFFHANGER
& HIS JR. PARK RANGERS

MOUNTAIN RESCUE: PRESERVING OUR GREAT
SMOKY MOUNTAINS NATIONAL PARK

D1523182

MARK VILLAREAL

FOREWORD

Brock Cliffhanger is a legend as far as Park Rangers go. However, if you ask Brock, he always plays his legend status down. He is a humble man and this has served him well as his leadership in teaching others, leading others, and most importantly, serving others are paramount in his value system. Brock started as a young boy, loving the idea of one day becoming a Park Ranger. As a boy he studied the safety rules of being a Park Ranger. He became a Jr. Park Ranger where he learned from Park Rangers teaching their trade with care and precision, for the passing on of their craft and knowledge could one day save a life. Brock always appreciated the devotion that Park Rangers had in their beliefs, and he learned early on that the best Park Rangers pay it forward. Funny, but it seems like every Park Ranger is "the best" as they all seem to live by the motto of paying it forward. To the Jr. Park Rangers that know Brock, he is larger than life, as well as larger than any challenge there is. In fact, to hear them speak of Brock, you would imagine that he towers above the trees and the mountains.

A park ranger, park warden or forest ranger is a person entrusted with protecting and preserving parklands—national, state, provincial or local parks. Although the first National Parks began in 1872, the first Park Rangers began in 1905. Prior to 1905 the military was assigned to the National Parks, but then the number and popularity of National Parks grew. On August 25, 1916 the formation of the National Parks Service was created. However, the term Ranger does date back to 1898 for the three parks in California that were National Parks and the individuals that stayed behind year round were called Rangers. The Rangers live the values to serve and protect, and to follow the guidelines of safety and common sense. Brock Cliffhanger is the very example of the values set forth, along with honesty, integrity, trust, respect, and most of all, humility.

Brock had earned a reputation of serving the community and the very National Parks that he was assigned to. His desire was for everyone's safe enjoyment of the National Parks. Brock wanted to pay it forward and educate, as all Park Rangers do. It is with this hope and blessing that he has mentored Jr. Park Rangers that, as like him, are the ones to carry on the craft of a Park Ranger and the love of caring for people and the State and National Parks. Brock loves to see the passion in the young Jr. Park Rangers' hearts and the excitement in their eyes. However, like his own mentor, Brock teaches with patience knowing that true learning takes time and effort. Every aspect of safety can save a life, so paying attention and following instructions are important. Brock now travels to different State and National Parks around the United States to spread the word on the importance of protecting our Parks. He brings two of his Jr. Park Rangers, Jack and Warren on several of his trips to assist in teaching others and with tasks of the day. Jack and Warren are brothers, with Jack being the older brother who became a Jr. Park Ranger first. With love and care, he has participated in teaching his brother. Together, they set out to live the Park Ranger motto of paying it forward.

Brief History Of The Great Smoky Mountains National Park:

The Great Smoky Mountains National Park is an American national park that straddles the ridgeline of the Great Smoky Mountains and part of the Blue Ridge Mountains, which are a division of the larger Appalachian Mountain chain. The border between Tennessee and North Carolina runs northeast to southwest through the centerline of the park. The Great Smoky Mountains is the most visited national park in the United States, with over 11.3 million recreational visitors in 2016. The Appalachian Trail passes through the center of the park on its route from Maine to Georgia. The park was chartered by the United States Congress in 1934 and officially dedicated by President Franklin D. Roosevelt in 1940.

The park encompasses 522,419 acres making it one of the largest protected areas in the eastern United States. Before the arrival of European settlers, the region was part of the homeland of the Cherokees. 1,000 years ago, Cherokee lived in the Great Smoky Mountains until 1838 when the US Government resettled them in Oklahoma. Frontier people began settling the land in the 18th and early 19th century. In 1830 President Andrew Jackson signed the Indian Removal Act, beginning the process that eventually resulted in the forced removal of all Indian tribes east of the Mississippi River to what is now Oklahoma. Many of the Cherokee left, but some, led by renegade warrior Tsali, hid out in the area that is now the Great Smoky Mountains National Park. Some of their descendants now live in the **Qualla Boundary** to the south of the park.

The Cherokee called the Great Smoky Mountain area "Land of the Blue Smoke", but that smoke is actually better described as mist or fog. The mist is formed by all of the vapor given off by the millions of trees, bushes and other vegetation in the mountains. The fog takes on a blueish appearance because the vapor molecules scatter the blue light from the sky.

As white settlers arrived, logging grew as a major industry in the mountains, and a rail line, the Little River Railroad, was constructed in the late-19th Century to haul timber out of the remote regions of the area. Cut-and-run-style clearcutting was destroying the natural beauty of the area, so visitors and locals banded together to raise money for preservation of the land. The U.S. National Park Service wanted a park in the eastern United States, but did not have much money to establish one. Though Congress had authorized the park in 1926, there was no authority of federally owned land around which to build a park. John D. Rockefeller, Jr., contributed $5 million, the U.S. government added $2 million, and private citizens from Tennessee and North Carolina pitched in to assemble the land for the park, piece by piece. Slowly, mountain homesteaders, miners, and loggers were evicted from the land. Farms and timbering operations were abolished to establish the protected areas of the park. Travel writer Horace Kephart, for whom Mount Kephart was named, and photographers Jim Thompson and George Masa were instrumental in fostering the development of the park. Former Governor Ben W. Hooper of Tennessee was the principal land purchasing agent for the park, which was officially established in 1934. (1)

Notes: (1)—Wikipedia

JR. PARK RANGER TRAINING

Brock and the boys arrived at the Great Smoky Mountain Ranger Station at Cades Cove in the late afternoon. Brock was thrilled with excitement, although the boys did not know why. Jack and Warren were excited as the Smoky Mountains were near and dear to their heart. They studied about all State and National Parks, but the Great Smoky Mountains drew their attention as it was vast and had a unique history to tell. They enjoyed reading tales of the past, its wildlife, the environment, and would spend hours reviewing pictures from books and magazines. That is why it disturbed them deeply when the forest fires of 2016 broke out and caused damage and hardship to the park, wildlife and local residents. This is part of the reason for their excitement to come see the park, and teach and work with others on its preservation. Brock introduced the boys to several of the Park Rangers on duty and then he guided them to an area across the road built for outdoor presentations. Brock and the boys made their way across the road and they went to the pavilion area where other kids their age and many parents were waiting for the event. There was a small staging area with a podium and table with handouts. In addition, there was a bulletin board to display training materials for the presentation. Brock appeared as excited as the boys.

Brock and the boys found seats. Jack read out loud the name of the event listed on the bulletin board, "7 Principles of Leave No Trace." Warren questioned what it was about. Brock shrugged his shoulders as if he did not know and was curious himself. As Jack started to take a guess, that is when the presenter came out. The crowd settled down to show respect to the presenter and to hear what he was about to say.

"Hello everyone," said the Park Ranger that entered the pavilion. He was an older gentlemen with an aura of gentleness about him. Everyone said hello in reply. "My name is Park Ranger Roger Wayne Corey. I have been a Park Ranger for the National Park Services for 27 years. Welcome to today's event of 7 Principles of Leave No Trace. We here at the Great Smoky Mountains National Park love what we do. To interact with guests like yourself, and most of all, of living and taking care of the Great Smoky Mountains National Park. We, like you, believe we are guests to the National Park, and as a good guest it is important to know how to act while visiting. That is what we are to learn about today. As most of you are aware, in 2016 we had a large forest fire here in the park and that makes it more important to teach and learn the fundamentals of preserving the park's natural state and leaving it as we found it."

Everyone seemed excited—Jack, Warren, and especially, Brock. Jack wondered why Brock was excited as he was so well versed in everything about the National Parks and the rules of preservation. At that moment, both Jack and Warren realized why. Park Ranger Corey stopped and said with excitement, "Well, we are in for a treat today. Boys and girls, and parents in the audience, today we have one of my students of many years ago who started as a Jr. Park Ranger, like each of you. He pursued his dream of becoming a Park Ranger, worked and studied hard and has become a leader of our industry as well as a legend to all of us. Ladies and gentlemen, I present to you, Brock Cliffhanger."

Brock stood up and waved. He actually seemed a little embarrassed, which was funny for the boys as they had never seen him that way before. Park Ranger Corey walked over as the audience was clapping and shook Brock's hand, but as they were shaking hands Brock pulled him closer for a hug.

"Great to see you. You know I love you my friend." Brock stated.

"Yes, I do, and the same here my friend. I am always so happy to see you," replied Park Ranger Corey. "Let's talk after the event. I would love to meet your Jr. Park Rangers that you've brought with you."

Brock acknowledged that they would stay after the event. Jack and Warren now understood why Brock was so excited. He spoke of so many mentors that have mentored him throughout the years. In fact, he teaches the boys to have mentors, and to seek mentors that share the right values and qualities. Brock believes good mentors are important. He believes that when you have good mentors as a youth, you are then encouraged to mentor others when you get older. The boys had heard Brock's stories of his mentors, but he always spoke highly of the one mentor that taught him early in his Jr. Park Rangers days. The boys now realized that this was Park Ranger Corey. The boys, Jack and Warren, hold Brock in the highest regard and see him as larger than life. So for Park Ranger Corey to be one of Brock's mentors, they realized how special he must be. They can see how Brock loves and appreciates this man just from the short interaction they witnessed. They were in awe of Park Ranger Corey and were inspired to learn what he was about to teach.

"Wow, this was the Park Ranger that taught Brock when he was in the Jr. Park Ranger Program!" Jack whispered in Warren's ear. Warren's eyes opened wider with excitement.

Park Ranger Corey went back to the small podium and proceeded with his presentation. "Thanks, everyone. I want to talk to you about Leave No Legacy, Leave No Trace Behind." Park Ranger Corey pointed to the title on the bulletin board. He further explained, "This means a commitment, a commitment from me, a commitment from you, and hopefully a commitment from everyone that visits our beautiful park. We want everyone to experience its beauty and to see all of its natural elements. How many here are willing to make this commitment?" he asked.

Everyone raised their hands enthusiastically. "Great, I am glad to see that! I ask because it is more than a verbal commitment. At times it is a physical commitment, as well. But we all want to enjoy the National Park. To do so we must commit to leaving the back country the same way we found it. This is how we show respect for others, but just as important, this is how we show respect for the park." Everyone nodded their heads in agreement. Park Ranger Corey continued. "Very good, now let's proceed. Here are the 7 Principles of Leave No Trace Behind. These are principles to follow that include safety, as well as conservation methods to preserve our park for our visitors, but also for our wildlife. So Principle #1 is, Know Before You Go, have an all planning map." Park Ranger Corey had these words written on a card that he then hung up on the bulletin board. "Why would this be important? Raise your hand if you know."

About five kids raised their hands. Park Ranger Corey selected a young girl near the back row. "It is important because you need to know where you are going to go so you do not get lost." she answered.

"Great answer!" exclaimed Park Ranger Corey. "That is correct. You need to plan before you go, and communicate your plan to others who are not going on your trip. An all planning map, shows all of the trails and allows you to also understand where you are, and recognize where you are going. Here is a scary fact about Clingmans Dome. This area is so large, that it can take eight Rangers to find you if you are missing. This is because there are so many ways in and so many ways out. This is why communicating to someone else about your plans is very important as well. If you find yourself lost, you may run low on food or the weather may change and leave you stuck in the elements. This is why I carry an all planning map, but I also protect it in a zip lock storage bag. I would not want to have something happen to it." Park Ranger Corey held up a clear plastic storage bag and placed his map into the bag and closed it up for demonstration.

"Okay, so Principle #2 is Stick To The Trails & Camp Overnight Right." He held up the card with this information written on it and hung it on the clip board underneath Principle #1. "Principle #1 is about a map and planning, but Principle #2 speaks to the importance of sticking to the trails. It is too easy to assume straying off a trail is okay as long as you can still see the trail. But each time you do it, you tend to stray a little more. But even a little can be dangerous. Each year we encounter people who stray away from the trail and then get hurt and cannot be seen. Staying on the trails allows us to find you quicker, and more importantly allows you to find each other. About two years ago, a woman who had hiked here many times separated from her daughter and disappeared to where the daughter could not find her. The daughter made it back to our station, but it took days to find her mother who became injured after straying off a trail and then perished. I don't mean to scare you, but I do mean to educate you. Each of you are important to us," he stated. "Now what do I mean about Camp Overnight Right?"

Several kids raised their hands. Park Ranger Corey chose a young boy who was sitting near the front. The boy stood up when selected and answered, "I believe you mean to follow the rules when camping overnight."

"Great answer!" replied Park Ranger Corey. "It does mean to follow the rules. There are several rules," continued Park Ranger Corey as he held up a pamphlet that read, Safe Camping Rules. "There are several rules, all meant for your safety. There are rules on where you camp, when you camp and how you camp. There are rules on camp fires, how you start them and how you control them. There are especially rules on how you store your food, trash handling and disposal and when you need to go to the restroom. How many knew there are that many rules?"

Only a few of the audience raised their hands. "That is why we have a guide. No matter how experienced you believe you are, you should always carry a guide. I carry a guide with me at all times. I also keep this in my zip lock bag to keep it protected from the elements. How you camp is important, as you do not want to attract wildlife. But you also want to leave your campsite in good, safe condition."

Jack and Warren were enjoying the presentation. Jack liked taking notes, even though he was already knowledge-able within the topic. To him it was important for him to learn from others and how they teach the subject matter. This has taught him different styles and techniques on how other Park Rangers teach and this makes him a better Jr. Park Ranger. He has learned to utilize their stories at times when the situations would present itself.

Park Ranger Corey continued, "Principe #3, Dispose of Your Trash and Pick up Your Animal Poop. The Ranger Station has plastic bags for animal poop. Consider carrying a one gallon, or larger, zip lock bag to pick up trash you encounter." He then gave some examples about the breakdown of human trash. "If you throw a half-eaten apple down it takes one month to decompose. A paper bag takes a month and a half to decompose. A cotton handkerchief takes 5 months to decompose. A wool sock takes one year. A tin can takes 90 years to decompose. Bones take 100 years—chicken and ribs, and other edible animal bones. Glass bottles take 200 years to decompose. Plastic bottles last forever, they never decompose. A styrofoam cup lasts forever." He held up a styrofoam cup for everyone to comprehend. People use Styrofoam cups so often that this information was insightful and made an impact when he showed examples. Jack thought this was very effective. Park Ranger Corey finished by saying, "Your animal is not natural to our parks, what they eat is different from local wildlife. Therefore their poop is not natural and other animals can smell it, be attracted to it, and even become ill from it. Carry poop bags to bag and dispose your pets poop properly."

Park Ranger Corey hung up the card for Principle #3 and continued. "Now Principle #4 is Leave It As You Found It. Don't pick flowers or move rocks. Let everyone enjoy things as they are, in their natural environment. Why would this be important?"

Only a couple of kids raised their hands. Park Ranger Corey chose one to answer. She stood up and replied, "Because we want everyone to enjoy the beauty of nature and how and where things grow."

"That is a good answer!" responded Park Ranger Corey. "Certainly, we want everyone to enjoy the landscape, the flowers and plants. But everything is sensitive, and affects other things as well." Park Ranger Corey picked up a flyer and read. "Almost all wildflowers are fragile and many wilt and perish soon after being picked. Over the years, the repercussions of wildflower picking by unthinking people, meaning inconsiderate, go far beyond the loss of the flowers themselves. A critical chain of events is triggered for years to come once wildflowers are lost. We don't often realize it, but wildflowers support entire ecosystems for pollinators, birds and small animals on a micro scale. Butterflies and other insects, small birds and animals depend on seeds, nectar and pollen for their food supply and life support system. In addition, some pollinators are not very mobile or have very small home ranges or depend on just one species of plant and die once their habitat has been destroyed." As he set the paper down, he continued, "You see, even if just a few people pick flowers or plants, soon those would die and affect other life species. In addition it becomes a problem, as some flowers or plants are rare, and visitors like them because they cannot find them elsewhere.

But by their selfishness we have seen some of these flowers or plants become non-existent from theft and damage."

Park Ranger Corey then picked up a printed flyer and read, "This is from the USDA, which is the United States Department of Agriculture, and they state there are four main consequences to the illegal activity of picking wildflowers or plants:

- All living organisms need to reproduce. Digging up wildflowers, picking wildflowers, or collecting their seed will reduce a plant's ability to reproduce and will adversely affect its long-term survival in that location;
- Removing wildflowers from the wild can adversely affect pollinators and other animals that depend on that species for food and cover;
- Removing wildflowers from our national forests and grasslands prevents other visitors from enjoying our natural heritage; and,
- Most wildflowers when dug from their natural habitat do not survive being transplanted.

Hopefully this helps. We need to be responsible to nature and let everyone enjoy the beauty that surrounds us." He hung up the card for Principle #4, and took a pause to drink some water.

Park Ranger Corey continued, "Principle #5, Be Careful With Fire. Build fire in a fire ring and make sure all fires burn to ashes. If you are camping in the backcountry, build small fires and allow them to burn down to ashes. Then in the morning spread the ashes around. Most of you are aware that recently we had a very large forest fire that caused a lot of damage. A lot of fires are started from carelessness or neglect from following these rules."

"How come you spread the ashes around in the morning?" asked a young man.

"One, you want to make sure the fire is totally out. The morning allows for that extra time. Also, burned wood does not contain nitrogen which has its harmful elements. But it does provide phosphorous, potassium, calcium, boron and other elements that growing plants need. So it supplies nutrients to the plants. This also allows ash not be blown around or to be breathed in," Park Ranger Corey explained.

Park Ranger Corey displayed the card for Principle #5 and continued, "Principle #6, Keep Wildlife Wild. Animals will try to stay away and move if you get too close. They may also growl to warn you. Animals are natural survivors and yet, beautiful as well. Don't let their beauty fool you. Furthermore, if they feel threatened they may attack. Especially if they have cubs around, they will naturally protect them. Finally, we want to keep forest animals dependent on nature and not us. They need the ability to hunt and find the natural food within the forest. Animals that become less afraid of humans may have to be put down, and this is sad because this can be avoided."

Park Ranger Corey paused to see that everyone understood that message. He then added to the display the card for

Principle #6 and proceeded. "Principle #7, Share Our Trails and Manage Your Pet. Animals must be on a leash. It is not just about if your pet is well trained. But wildlife is roaming around freely. We want to keep animals separated. Domesticated and wild mean two different things and we want to keep it that way. You cannot control or protect your animal if it is not on a leash. Unleashed animals may be viewed as a danger or prey, or may run into a dangerous situation. If you are following your animal, that can create danger for you too." Park Ranger Corey finished and posted the card for Principle #7. He then asked the crowd to reread each principle. He would call out the principle number and as a group they would respond with the answer and description of each principle. Everyone seemed excited to participate.

"Now let's review what items we should take when we go hiking. I have a list of items that I take and recommend. Number one, a backpack. Obviously I need something that I will carry my important items in, but not be burdensome to me. Here is what I bring in my backpack." Park Ranger Corey pulled out a list of numbered items and displayed them on the bulletin board, then started naming them in the following order.

1. Water—A little more than what you may calculate as needed.
2. Food, if it's a day hike take energy snacks that help restore energy.

3. Map, as we spoke about in our principles. Take extra in case you may be hiking with someone else.

4. A small shovel, and keep it in a plastic bag. This allows you to bury your poop properly.

5. Handy wipes, for cleaning messes and yourself.

6. Hand sanitizer, which is an antibacterial solution to clean your hands.

7. Toilet paper, for obvious reasons.

8. An emergency blanket to warm someone who might be injured.

9. Wear a whistle, that is louder than your voice can holler.

10. A small first aid kit in case of injury or scratches.

11. Headlamp, in case you are out after dark or are looking into something that needs light.

12. Trash bag, to clean up your messes as well as others.

13. Water filter & cup to filter and drink water from creeks.

14. Compass, to assist in directions when needed.

15. Handkerchief, which can help with injuries.

16. Copy of your latest physical in a plastic bag from your doctor. This has a list of prescriptions and health conditions in case you need medical attention.

What a great list. Jack and Warren took notes and appreciated the additional information they learned. Having a copy of your physical was a new and smart idea, especially for those hikers of older age or with medical conditions. Park Ranger Corey asked if there were any questions. There were a few questions from both youth and adults of which he answered. After answering, he announced that was the end of the session. He also announced to those in the Jr. Park Ranger Program, that they would receive credit for attending the session, and that he would sign their attendance card. Many stayed behind to have their cards signed for credit. Park Ranger Corey also took several pictures with the kids

Park Ranger Corey and young attendee.

and adults. Many just wanted to show their appreciation and shake Ranger Corey's hand. He appreciated their kind words. This seems to be what motivates Park Rangers, or at least a part of it. Making a difference and teaching others, especially youth is important. Park Rangers make great role models as they demonstrate the values we want our youth to learn.

As the attendees departed, Park Ranger Corey started to gather his items with the assistance from a helper. Brock walked over and started helping as well. This took only a few seconds and then Brock spoke. "Allow me to introduce you to my Jr. Park Rangers that traveled with me," he stated.

Park Ranger Corey walked a few steps over and said, "Let me guess, Jack and Warren."

The boys seemed surprised that he knew their names. "You remembered, I am impressed!" Brock exclaimed.

"Of course I remember," Ranger Corey replied. "You speak and write about them so much I feel like I know them so well. It is a pleasure to meet you both." he addressed the boys, as he extended his hand to shake Warren's and then Jack's hands. The boys said thanks, but seemed a little shy, which was unusual for both of them.

"These boys have done well in the program. We came to learn lessons about the forest fire here in 2016, and how to prevent them of course, but also what to do afterwards. Taking care of our parks and their ecosystem is important. Jack and Warren have such an appreciation for our parks and feel a special interest in the Great Smoky Mountains and their history," Brock stated.

"Yes, they were devastating, and a big challenge," declared Ranger Corey. "With hard work, a lot of prayer and skill, we eventually got them under control. God always comes through." Park Ranger Corey then directed the conversation to talk with Jack and Warren. "Boys, I knew Brock when he was young like you. He was anxious to learn, but sometimes a little too eager."

"I was a little too eager, wasn't I!?" Brock laughed. "You see boys, what Park Ranger Corey means is, as a youth I sometimes would want to rush to do things, or not listen carefully before taking action. I am sure that sometimes I simply believed I already knew what I needed to know. It is Park Ranger Corey who taught me to Stop, Look and Listen."

Jack and Warren both rolled their eyes and chuckled. They had a hard time imagining Brock as a child, or him not being a good listener. But they did know about Stop, Look and Listen, and obviously this was something Ranger Brock had taught them. It was also something he had to utilize several times with them. "How long did you have Ranger Brock in your program?" asked Warren.

Ranger Corey spoke, "When he was your age, probably two and a half years. I saw his growth then, and also when he was in his teenage years. Of course you may know we have worked together at some of the same parks, or when an emergency occurred that brought us together as well. Brock saved my life once when I was injured, as he brought me out of danger and to safety. You see boys, our motto is to always pay it forward. Sometimes when we pay it forward we never know when it might circle back. You cannot imagine the pride I felt when I watched Brock use his training and instincts when saving me." Ranger Corey patted Brock on his back as an expression of love and appreciation.

Brock spoke up, "Boys, I know you remember my stories of my first mentor in the Jr. Park Rangers." He looked toward Ranger Corey and stated, "Ranger Corey was that mentor. In some ways I was a little troubled as a youth and needed direction. Ranger Corey showed guidance, but discipline as well. Most of all he showed love and acceptance, which is what I needed at that time. It is because of him that I continued to pursue being a Park Ranger. Ranger Corey was my hero and who I looked up to. He was larger than life then, and still is larger than life to me now."

The boys stood in awe as Brock described Ranger Corey exactly how they viewed Brock. The boys did know that in some ways Brock was a troubled youth. They have heard Brock share this with others as a lesson to help them. But to see and meet Brock's mentor and hero was really something. By Jack and Warren witnessing how having a mentor to learn from, and then becoming a mentor to others, can come full circle, was a valuable lesson to learn.

"Can we get some pictures together?" asked Jack.

"Absolutely!" Ranger Corey replied joyfully.

The boys, Brock and Ranger Corey took several pictures in many different settings. Then they assisted Ranger

Corey in walking back across the road to the Ranger Station. Ranger Corey gave the boys a tour of the station and introduced them to other Rangers and staff. Of course many of the Rangers knew Brock, but not all. As Ranger Corey introduced them to Brock, they all had heard his name and were excited to meet him.

"Where are you off to now?" Ranger Corey asked.

"We need to set up our campsite for the evening," Brock answered. "Tomorrow we will attend the session on the 2016 forest fire, from which I am sure we will learn a lot of valuable information."

"Yes, you will. Ranger Johnson will be delivering that session," Ranger Corey informed them. "He has great slides, video and talking points. The boys will learn a lot. Well, best wishes to you and God Bless." Ranger Corey extended his hand for a handshake with Brock. He patted the boys on the back as they said thank you and goodbye to him.

Brock, Jack and Warren stopped at the small store by the campsite to purchase some items and then went to find their campsite location. They set up their tent and sleeping bags and then stayed up talking for a while and did some reading before the boys dozed off to sleep. Ranger Brock toured the campsite and walked through a mental checklist out of habit, to make sure everything was okay before going to bed.

The next morning came quickly, as it always seems to. With camping, the sunrise seems to be your alarm clock. Brock and Jack both wake up naturally with the sunlight, but

Warren seems to have a way to sleep through it as he is a deep sleeper. Sometimes Jack would play small tricks on Warren because he would sleep in, but not this morning. He simply woke up Warren as Brock had a small breakfast ready for them. They ate and then prepared for the day. Soon they were on their way to the Sugarland Visitors Center, where the event was to be held. The center was about a 20-minute drive from their camping location.

As they drove, the boys continued to take in the majestic beauty of the Great Smoky Mountains. They noticed the magnificent view when they arrived and now they could see it from a different direction and route. The Park was beautiful and it seems that there was always a running stream next to the road. At some points, the trees on both sides of the road formed a tunnel with their overhanging branches and provided shade as they drove through. The hillsides were lush with trees and plants and displayed different shades in color. Soon they arrived at the Sugarland Visitors Center which was much larger than the Ranger Station at the Cades Cove Campsite entrance. As they entered, there was a large gift shop and even a movie theater that showed a recurring movie on the Great Smoky Mountains. The boys noticed as they were entering, posted signs and directions to different hiking trails and sites for visitors to explore. Oh yes, the Great Smoky Mountains has it all, with so much to discover for everyone.

Brock brought the boys into a room set up for a small presentation. Others arrived and the boys met other Jr. Park

Rangers that were there to learn from the event as well. There were handouts on a table that Brock brought to Jack and Warren. Brock spoke with other Park Rangers who brought a few of their Jr. Park Rangers as the group found places to sit down. It was exciting for Jack and Warren, as they always enjoyed meeting with other Jr. Park Rangers and to witness that wherever they traveled there are young boys and girls that take such an interest in State and National Parks. Jack and Warren have a younger, curious sister that they mentor. In another year, they are looking forward to her joining the Jr. Park Ranger Program. She admires her brothers, and takes a keen interest in learning from them. This is very common in the Jr. Park Ranger Program with brothers and sisters making it a family affair.

It seemed everyone had arrived for the event, the start time was just a few minutes away, and Park Ranger Johnson made his entrance.

"Hello everyone!" Park Ranger Johnson boomed. "I am Park Ranger Johnson. I have been a Park Ranger for 21-years and experienced many wildfires. Today, we are going to talk about the wildfires we had here in the Great Smoky Mountains in 2016, their cause, how they spread and the aftermath. The biggest part of this lesson will show, that no matter how a fire may start, there are other elements that can cause it to spread. Certainly there are times when we do controlled fires, which are done to manage the ecosystem. But when fires start by accident or on purpose they can spread quickly before being reported. Once reported, other circumstances can come into play that makes it difficult for us to gain control. Such circumstances occurred with the wildfires of 2016. Let's get started."

As the lights were dimmed, Park Ranger Johnson started to show his slide presentation. "The wildfires in the Great Smoky Mountains started on November 23, 2016 originating at the Chimney Tops Trail, on Chimney Tops Mountain. Monte Le Conte is located east of Chimney Tops. Mount Mingus is southeast of the Chimney Tops and is practically walled in on all three sides. This fire, unfortunately, was man made in which two juveniles were arrested for starting it. This is sad, as we all care for this area, and for the many that were affected from this wildfire. From the start of the fire and over a few days that followed, water was dropped on the fire to assist in the containment. The fire was within its containment boundaries. However, humidity was around 17% as this was a period of exceptional drought. On or around November 27 and 28, winds picked up to around 40 miles per hour which drove the fire to spread outside the containment boundaries and to places such as the Chimney Top Picnic area and further north to a residential area known a Mynatt Park." As he was talking, Park Ranger Johnson was showing slides that showed both the areas, while on fire, and some pictures of the aftermath and the charred remains.

Park Ranger Johnson continued, "Soon winds picked up to as high as 87 miles per hour and wind driven sparks spread the fires to areas of Gatlinburg and Pigeon Forge. The wind knocked down trees which then knocked down power lines that started and spread additional fires. This is what is believed to have started a separate fire in the Cobby Nob Subdivision east of Gatlinburg. Because of power outages to some pumping stations, and because they burnt and caused damage, hydrants went dry. The damage also caused a lack of communications from cell phones as the radio system became overloaded. The fire even affected the 911 system in Gatlinburg as the operations system lost power. You can see how one circumstance can then affect another, which caused the fire to spread and responses to become difficult. Item one, a fire intentionally set. Item two, drought and dry conditions. Item three, winds that pick up and spread the fire. Item four, wind that knocked down power lines which then knocks out power to resources like water from the pumping station to communications. The downed power lines then sparks more fires and the fire grows."

The pictures were devastating to see, and the room was quiet and somber. The pictures showed the downed power lines, the charred picnic area and residential areas affected. There were pictures of the damaged pumping stations, and many pictures of the hard working men and women of the Forestry Department working the lines while battling the fires. Park Ranger Johnson emphasized, "The human factor was that 14 lives were lost. There were 134 reported injuries, as the fire was one of the largest natural disasters in the history of the state of Tennessee. There were over 2,400 buildings that were destroyed and 17,904 acres that burned. Obviously an event like this has a large effect on wildlife as well as the economy of the local towns that rely on tourism." Park Ranger Johnson paused for a moment, and took a drink of water. He allowed time for the pictures and the data to sink in and to take effect on the audience. The room was quiet as Jack and Warren clearly, like the other attendees, understood the dangers and consequences of fires. The session then took a ten minute break.

The boys mingled with some of the other Jr. Park Rangers in attendance. Each were moved by what the slide shows revealed on the damage and the circumstance of how it spread. As a Jr. Park Ranger, you have such an appreciation for the State and National Parks. Situations like a wildfire are heartbreaking. But this is why they became Jr. Park Rangers, to learn and educate others. To protect and preserve our parks is important so everyone can share the beauty. Jack and Warren also wanted to see some of the other programs that were being conducted that day. Both Jack and Warren were taking some Jr. Park Rangers on a hike through some of the trails that were in the wildfire to review with the group how vegetation and wildlife were affected, how they were being revived and to discuss the effects on wildlife when wildfires occur. Jack and Warren always want to see what other Jr. Park Rangers were learning or wanting to learn next. As they visit other parks with Jr. Park Rangers, they have become aware of other great ideas to add to programs which they share with

Brock and other leaders. Soon the break was over and it was time for the workshop session to continue.

Park Ranger Johnson came back into the room and restarted his slide presentation. He announced that he was going to review the day's agenda for the group. After this session, groups were separated to deliver different tours and prepare for their lessons. Brock, with Jack and Warren, were taking a group to some walking trails to review the area, and to discuss about how those areas and all other areas are recovering. Jack and Warren were also to discuss how wildfires affect wildlife during and after the fire. The boys studied for their part very thoroughly and were excited to share their knowledge with others. There were some other great tours and lessons to be delivered. One group was going up the Anakeesta lift, which is a ski lift-style ride they call "Chondola" that rides to the top of a mountain, and has awesome scenic views. These views also show how close the wildfires were to the town and other parts of the forest that were burned. There is also great entertainment there like dueling ziplines, a treehouse bridge, a forest walk and more. Another group was riding the Ober Aerial Tramway which travels 2.1 miles up the mountain and offers a 360 degree view of the Great Smoky Mountains and foothills. The other groups were exploring trails that would include stops to Newfound Gap and Gatlinburg Bypass Overlook. Mount LeConte and other key areas were being explored and discussed, with safety being the first priority. The groups were to meet back in the early evening for the group leaders to provide brief summaries of their group event and all attendees would enjoy a cook out. This was always a lot of fun as the Jr. Park Rangers always look forward to the exploration, learning and the cookouts together. The meeting was adjourned and Brock went to meet and gather together with the group he was leading today.

Brock, Jack and Warren met at the small bus that was available to take their group to their trail. Although this was a group of eight experienced Jr. Park Rangers, Brock always went through the safety steps and checklist. It starts with counting that everyone is present and that each Jr. Park Ranger is prepared. Obviously the list may vary based upon conditions like weather, altitude and time of day, although being prepared for the unexpected is always a plus and a priority of their planning. Brock checked that each participant had their backpack, weather appropriate clothing, hiking boots or shoes, food, water, maps and compass, first aid essentials and a knife or multi tool. There are more items that can be brought, so Brock and the boys always bring extra supplies with them. Brock likes to teach using Park Ranger Corey's list. He sent the list out to all Jr. Park Rangers who signed up for this hike weeks prior to the scheduled event. Brock also reviewed several of the rules with each participant being responsible for a partner as well. Each Jr. Park Ranger had their caps to wear, as well as knitted beanie's to change into if the weather became cooler. Brock asked for silence as he spoke a prayer for the day and for the group which was customary for Brock, as he is a man of faith. The prayer was completed and the bus started their journey. The group left with excitement.

As the bus started driving, Jack introduced the bus driver, Park Ranger Bronson, and then led the group in fun discussions, trivia and games. He asked for each Jr. Park Ranger to introduce themselves, their background and to tell a brief story about themselves. He and Warren then had a contest where Jack would ask questions and Warren would announce who the winner was and award the prize. They had neat little prizes, such as guides or small equipment items that Jr. Park Rangers enjoy. They then sang a few songs, with Brock's voice coming through strong, which made a few of the youth laugh, but it was all in fun. The bus ride was not too long. The bus was loud, as you can imagine a bus filled with youth would be. They all enjoyed the program and are always excited about the pending event. At this moment, Brock asked the group to quiet down. He wanted to review some standard rules that he knows each Jr. Park Ranger knows, but Park Rangers are always taught to constantly review safety. He once again spoke about being responsible for your partner, but sometimes things happen. He then reminded them of the STOP Rule.

"Remember, if for any reason you get lost, remember the STOP Rule.

- Stop, as soon as you realize that you are lost!
- Think, how did you get to where you are?

- Observe what you can see.
- Plan, never move until you have a plan.

We all know this as the STOP Rule."

Brock paused and opened his map. "Now, this is a map of the trail. Everyone please open your map." He waited as each Jr. Park Ranger located their map, pulled it out and opened it. "Now, we are starting on the trail at this point and walking this direction. So this would help with numbers two and three of the STOP rule. It will also help if we need to find you. Review the map carefully and use your compass when needed."

The Jr. Park Rangers listened and studied the map. They have been taught well and are used to redundancy for safety. A few marked their map with pencils to show the starting point and the direction of their hike. Brock spoke some more, "Now we definitely followed the safety list of what to do before going hiking. Who can remember the first four rules?"

Several raised their hands and he pointed at Sally. She lowered her hand and started naming them in order, "Number 1, avoid hiking alone and on unknown trails. Number 2, make sure to inform someone from outside your group about your route and schedule. Number 3, is to plan ahead. Number four, is to do your research." She stopped and caught her breath, as she was rattling them off very quickly.

Broke spoke up, "Sally, very good, now Park Ranger Johnson knows our plan and our route as does the Ranger Station. Our group is not too large, so it should be easy to stay together. When we stop to speak about an area or to take a break, we will also make sure everyone is with the group and aware that we are moving forward."

The bus came to a stop and Brock directed everyone to exit. He had Jack and Warren exit first and directed everyone to line up next to them. Brock exited last and joined the group. He explained that Jack and Warren will speak through several educational talking points throughout the hike, and asked everyone to pay attention as there would be a quiz on the subject matter. Brock explained, that because he is familiar with the trail, he will take the lead and for them to follow him in pairs. Brock reminded them that the trails around Cades Cove are listed as a moderate trail. This means the trail may have more inclines, hills and elevation changes, but should be manageable by anyone who is moderately active. Brock chose the Cades Cove Nature Trail as it would be manageable and allow the team to not encounter any strenuous inclines or difficulty. The Jr. Park Rangers that were selected had to have history of hiking this level of trail. But with a group of eight Jr. Park Rangers, two adults, Brock and the planning leaders always want to play it safe. To add to that safety, Park Ranger Bronson will be at the rear of the group to assist and help manage.

The group was gathered and ready to start. Warren asked if everyone was ready and if there were any questions before they begin. Billy, one of the Jr. Park Rangers, raised his hand.

"Yes, Billy, what question do you have?" Warren asked.

"Why can't we go to Chimney Tops where the fire started? Would that not show us a lot about the fire?" Billy asked.

Chimney Tops is a 3.8 mile round-trip hike and does have a portion with an extreme uphill incline. The trail ends at a newly constructed observation point overlooking Mount LeConte and the Pinnacles where you can feel the wilderness open to the wild. It is one of Brock's favorite hiking trails and it brought pain to him when the wilderness fire was occurring. He has told the boys so much about the different trails in the Great Smoky Mountains and they have looked forward to their visit. After today's hike, before him and the boys travel back home, he plans on taking the boys to Laurel Falls, but had already explained to them earlier that Chimney Tops was too challenging for this group. Laurel Falls is an easy trail, about a 2.6 miles round-trip trail that is paved. The trail leads to a beautiful cascading waterfall named for the mountain laurels that bloom along the trail.

"Chimney Tops has some strenuous areas that, for our group, would be too challenging. Remember, safety is our first priority. We will however talk about Chimney Tops and other areas of this trail and about their plants, trees and wildlife," Warren answered.

Brock was proud of the response. Jr. Park Rangers were always taught about safety, but they were youthful at heart, and youthfulness still makes them believe that nothing can harm them. This is why repetitiveness is always important. Human nature will have a tendency to show itself. The group started down the path as Brock led.

Just about 5 minutes of hiking, Jack stopped at a spot that showed a good view of vegetation of plants and trees. "There are more than 1,500 different flowers and plants throughout the Great Smoky Mountains," Jack stated. "There are also over 130 species of trees."

Warren then spoke up, "There are also more than 200 species of birds and 68 species of mammals. 67 native fish species, 39 species of reptiles and 43 species of amphibians, which are your frogs, toads and salamanders." Warren was reading from his clipboard on information he had prepared.

"What we are saying here," Jack continued, "is that the Great Smoky Mountains is unlike any other place. It has more diversity in plants, trees and animals than any other place. This is because of the different elevations, climate, mountains and weather. This is important as we all love and appreciate nature and our National Parks. So understanding each park and its unique aspects is important. Because when we do not protect them by educating others, bad things can happen like the forest fires. Small things can make an impact and not being educated can cause big problems."

The group was a little quiet, as they all love the National Parks and what they bring. Each of them have dreams of being a Park Ranger and want to live taking care of the parks and those that visit them. Their love and appreciation of the parks makes them take it personally. It drives them to learn. Brock, and the other leaders, understand that it is their responsibility to know how to instill that desire in the right manner and in a nurturing way.

Jack asked if there were any questions or comments from the group. Connor, one of the Jr. Park Rangers, raised his hand.

"Connor?" Jack said.

"Yes," he stated. "Why does the Great Smoky Mountains have more different species of plants, animals and trees? How did that come to be?"

"Connor, that is a great question," Jack replied. "One, because of different elevations, mountains, weather and climate at each level. This allows for the different species to flourish and survive in the areas where they grow or live best. Some animals or plants may flourish at a higher level and others at a lower level. The Copperhead Snake lives here in the Great Smoky Mountains, but below 3,000 feet. Yet, the Timber Rattler lives above 3,000 feet. Because the Great Smoky Mountains have so many different elevations it allows many different levels of wildlife, plants and trees to flourish."

Brock then spoke up, "There is also another reason on how they got here."

Brock caught the attention of the group with his statement and they all turned towards him, waiting for his explanation.

Brock explained, "I am sure each of you have heard of the ice age. Well, the Great Smoky Mountains are considered to be 200 to 300 million years old. The glaciers of the last ice age covered North America, except it did not cover the Great Smoky Mountains. So, the animals and plants found safety in the Great Smoky Mountains as the ice age drove them here, along with what other animals were already living here. Pretty amazing, isn't it?!"

The group all nodded their heads in amazement. Each time, whether at their events, or through their Jr. Park Rangers guides and lessons, they learn so much amazing information. Over time they see how small things have big effects and how things a long time ago have shaped many things of today. Brock's explanation of the ice age was one such item.

Jack motioned to the group and hollered, "Let's move down the trail some more." The group walked down the trail. There was some running water as well as other hikers and families on the trail. It is great to see the hiking trails and the park being explored and appreciated. Jack brought them by an area near some tall trees. There was also a camping area that could be seen from where they were with a sign that read, *Keep your firewood at home.*

Warren turned to the group and asked, "Who can answer why that sign says to keep your firewood at home?"

It seemed the whole group knew, as they have been taught well. Warren pointed to Jackson, a Jr. Park Ranger from North Carolina.

"Because insects from other areas hide in the firewood and then can come and cause damage to an area they did not originally live in," Jackson answered.

"Exactly!" Warren answered. Brock and Bronson had big smiles as they always enjoy and take pride in the growth and knowledge of young Jr. Park Rangers learning.

Jack then spoke up, "Look at these beautiful trees. Many of the trees in the Great Smoky Mountains are 150 to 400 years old. Yet, so many things can affect and attack them from wildfires to people. But by bringing firewood from the outside, you may bring an insect that is not common to the Great Smoky Mountains that will then spread itself in this area."

"Yes," Warren replied. "In Clingmans Dome you will see Fraser fir trees wiped out by a foreign insect not from this area."

"You are correct Warren, good job!" Brock praised. "This insect, known as the balsam woolly adelgid, arrived sometime in the 1960's and they feed on these trees. They have wiped out about ninety percent of the mature trees in that area. Now they are studying other Fraser firs in other areas that seem to be resistant, to see how they can stop this damage from spreading. If you looked around as we drove here, you should have seen many dead Hemlock trees. Those are being attacked by the hemlock woolly aldegid from East Asia. These trees play a role by keeping temperatures low in mountain streams and providing habitat for other species. Once again, you can see how one thing affects the other."

All stood in silence. Jack let that information sink in a little before speaking. You could see the Jr. Park Rangers shaking their heads in disbelief, and some looking up at the trees and around the forest. When one realizes the damage that is being done to the forest, they seem to appreciate it more.

Brock thought of another point to educate the Jr. Park Rangers on as the moment seemed appropriate. "In the late

1800's, logging companies were drawn to the Great Smoky Mountains. Logging companies would buy large acres of land, log all the trees and then sell the land. Overtime, the land that was now empty would have its top soil wash away when it would rain, which affected plants and the wildlife who depended on vegetation. This is why in the early 1900's concerned citizens wanted to protect the area. It is their efforts that eventually convinced the government to declare the Great Smoky Mountains a National Park. We have a lot to thank them for our park today."

Jack and Warren always appreciated when Brock educates everyone. They may have heard some of this before, but there is always so much to share. What is important to them is that everyone learns so that they can pay it forward.

"Ready to proceed, Jack?" Brock asked.

"Yes, let's walk further down." Jack then turned toward the group. "Let's go this way everyone." Jack waved his right arm forward and started walking. Everyone was enjoying the path, looking to each side. This was a well behaved group, which Brock and Bronson appreciated. They walked for a while, everyone staying together. They noticed an older man bending down, looking behind a tree off the trail with his camera. They moved quietly so they would not startle him or what he was looking at. As Jack arrived first, he saw the gentlemen was observing a woodpecker who was pecking on a small piece of a branch. Jack motioned for the others to move quietly and not rush towards the area. Warren then held out his hand and motioned as he instructed for two at a time to look around the tree and view. Jack would tap them on the shoulder when it was time for the next Jr. Park Rangers to take a glimpse. Jr. Park Rangers are taught to be respectful and appreciative of wildlife and to be protective of it. They would try not to startle any wildlife or chase it away, and they would keep a safe distance when encountering animals. Finally, it was important to let wildlife be wild. They would never provide food or ruin their habitat. They really appreciated the beauty of the woodpecker. They each had their view,

Woodpecker pecking on a branch.

and they then were motioned by Jack to walk farther down the path. The group hiked about another 45-minutes and Jack then stopped at some beautiful vegetation and wildflowers.

"Everything we have seen and discussed shows us how man and their actions can affect the National Park in a destructive way, like bringing firewood from the outside," Jack began to gain their attention. "It is important that we learn this as this is just one part of the dangers."

"Yes," Warren added. "Then think about all of those things that attack the National Parks and then a wildfire happens to attack it more."

"Exactly!" said Jack. "So when we hear of things that people do that cause damage and they just don't realize the harm, think about when they intentionally do things."

Jack had the groups' attention. What did he mean? Perhaps the wildfire that was arson?

"What I am talking about is people that pick the vegetation and flowers," Jack continued. "Each of us have learned not to even pick one flower as this can have repercussions. But there are people that come to actually steal the vegetation and flowers so they can either replant at home or use for a business. This actually happens."

"This is what we call plant poaching," added Brock. "Some commercial poachers remove hundreds of plants each trip. This, and careless hikers trampling over plants, along with individuals picking one at a time have a long term effect on the forest."

"This is why the leave no trace rule is important," said Warren. "Whatever you carry in, please carry out. Everything else is protected."

The group stood there admiring the plants and flowers in the area. Many of them could not believe that people would come and purposely steal plants and flowers to replant elsewhere and sell. As a young child, it is hard to understand the greed that individuals may have or the lack of concern of the harm that they may cause. It was time to hike a little more, so Jack signaled and whistled slightly to gain everyone's attention. Brock and Bronson ensured all were together.

Jack journeyed about 15 minutes or so, allowing the Jr. Park Rangers to enjoy the views from each side of the trail. There was plenty of vegetation, flowers and trees. There was also a running stream where they could all rest and enjoy the sound of the stream.

"What happens to the animals when a wildfire occurs?" asked Ana, one of the Jr. Park Rangers.

"They instinctually fight to survive," replied Brock. "In fact, Jack and Warren studied this and can answer a little more on the subject and about the animals here in the Great Smoky Mountains National Park. Boys, can you please share?"

"Animals have a strong sense of when things are wrong and it is their instinct to get away from it," Jack began. "Most, naturally try to move away from danger if they can. Birds will fly away. Mammals will run. Amphibians, like frogs, toads and salamanders and other small creatures will burrow into

Jr. Park Rangers Enjoying A Beautiful running stream.

the ground, hide out in logs or take cover under rocks. Large animals like elk will take refuge in streams and lakes."

Warren then chimed in, "Most animals have senses that alert them of the danger and they move on. The animals that burrow underground, do so and wait it out. I heard of one reported bear death in the Great Smoky Mountain wildfire, and there may have been more, but that is a low percentage."

"Exactly!" stated Brock. "In fact, there is an organization that has tagged many of the black bears here in the Great Smoky Mountains, and during the fire they were able to track their movement and could see that they were moving away from the fire as well as ahead of it. Certainly, some animals can get caught when the fire is being fueled by wind and other factors, but the animals are incredibly smart."

"I read that even when they have found fish that have died, that they more than likely died from the fire retardant or the ash that polluted their water," Jack contributed.

"Great point, Jack," said Brock. "Fires happen naturally as well, from lightning strikes, etc. Animals have learned to live and even flourish from fires too. In some ways even rely on them."

"How do they rely on them?" asked Randy, another young Jr. Park Ranger.

Brock responded, "Pine trees require the intense heat of a forest fire to open their cones and release their seeds. No fire, no new trees. A woodpecker and many types of quail, foxes, bears, squirrels and other animals depend on fire to keep undergrowth in check. Consequently, all forest-dwelling plants and animals have co-evolved with the inevitable fires and have found ways to adapt."

"Some species of bears have learned how to hunt and feed off of fleeing animals during a fire, so they instinctively know what the fire may cause in other animals," said Jack.

Ana asked, "Are the animals more dangerous when there is a wildfire?"

"We need to always treat animals with respect, as most animals will protect themselves if they feel they are in danger. Animals have natural survival instincts," answered Jack.

"Exactly!" commented Brock. "Think of it this way. In normal circumstances we teach to treat them with respect as if when they sense danger they may attack. Now intensify that with a fire or other disaster that has their senses even more sensitive. This is even more reason to stay clear of them."

The group of young Jr. Park Rangers took in the conversation shaking their heads and giving it some thought.

"What animals are dangerous in the Great Smoky Mountains?" Ana asked.

"That is something I have Warren cover when we take a group out to learn at any National Park," Brock answered. "Warren loves to study the different species at different State and National Parks. Warren?"

Warren was prepared, and pulled out a one page flyer he had created from his backpack and started reading. "All animals, large or small, need to be protected, respected and left undisturbed. If you see an animal in distress, report it to a Park Ranger." He paused, and then started reading some more. "From what I read, there are 10 animals that could kill if they wanted to in the Great Smoky Mountains. Number 1 is a bobcat. Bobcats usually keep to themselves and avoid contact. But they will, if concerned or felt threatened, they may attack."

"Yes!" amplified Brock. "Bobcats here can get up to seventy pounds. They hunt rabbits, rodents and birds. They would be rare to see because they keep to themselves."

Warren spoke again, "Number 2 is the eastern cougar. You may also know them as a puma."

"If you sight one of these, it would be a rare sighting as well," said Jack. "These animals can get up to one hundred and forty pounds, but they are generally shy. However, they have been known to have killed in the past."

"What is number 3, Warren?" Brock asked.

"Number 3 is a skunk," Warren replied. "Most of us know skunks will spray to protect themselves and their territory."

"Yes, and that smell is very hard to get rid of," Jack stated. "But the message here is that they could kill and should be considered dangerous."

Warren continued, "Number 4 is a black bear. Most of us would always think of all bears as dangerous. Black bears are smaller than other species of bears, so this may make us think they are less dangerous."

Jack spoke up, "Most of their time is spent looking for food. Black bears will be very protective of their young, so if you see a cub, expect that there is a mama bear around and don't get close. Black bears will eat human food which hurts their lifespan, but also might make them more comfortable around humans, which makes them dangerous."

"What is number 5, Warren?" Brock asked.

"Number 5 is a wild boar," Warren answered.

A Great Smoky Mountain Black Bear.

"A wild boar?" a few of the Jr. Park Rangers replied.

"Yes, a wild boar," Jack spoke up. "I know this is surprising, but wild boars are not natural to the Great Smoky Mountains. And yet, somehow they are here now."

Brock could tell that the Jr. Park Ranger group was intrigued and surprised that there were wild boars in the Great Smoky Mountains. "Listen," Brock said, "like all animals, give them respect. If you see one, walk away. Like black bears, they are very protective of their young."

"Don't boars have horns or tusks?" asked Billy, one of the Jr. Park Rangers.

"Yes," answered Brock. "Both male and female have tusks, but the males are longer. They have been known to charge when they feel danger or to defend their young. Females have been known to bite."

"Ready for number 6?" Warren asked.

The Jr. Park Ranger group nodded their head yes.

"Number 6 is a coyote," Warren continued.

"Don't coyotes look like dogs?" asked Billy.

"Yes, they do, but they have a round bushy tail," Jack answered.

"Yes, and the ones in the Great Smoky Mountains have thick dark fur with white bellies," Brock stated. "They are fast and can leap very high. They normally eat small prey, but will hunt larger prey when they travel in a pack."

"You can hear them howl at night," Jack added. "I am sure we all have heard them when camping."

The group nodded their heads in agreement, as each of them come with vast camping experience and have heard the howl of a coyote.

"Let's continue, Warren," Brock prompted.

"Okay," stated Warren. "Number 7 is a red fox. They are extremely shy and about the size of a dog."

"They are beautiful animals," Jack replied. "They have a rust color and a fluffy tail."

"Jack is correct," Brock stated. "All of these animals are beautiful in their own way. But like other animals, a red fox will eat human food, which draws them closer to humans and can make them dangerous."

"We are now on number 8," Warren announced. "Number 8 is the red wolves. They can be red, grey, yellow or black."

"Listen," Brock spoke up. "The red wolves are an endangered species. I believe they estimate there may be only 350 left in the world!" Brock paused to let that sink in. "In this park, they estimate about twenty five of them that live here. They are also shy, so it would be rare to see one. They normally eat on raccoons or groundhogs." Brock then motioned to Warren, "Continue please."

"Number 9 would be the copperhead snake," Warren continued. "As we all know, this is a poisonous snake. They are typically copper, orange or pinkish in color."

"Yes," Jack said. "This is probably one of the most common snake bites in the U.S."

"That is correct, Jack," Brock confirmed. "Part of it is because they are more common below 3,000 feet. They will strike when threatened. Now we all must wear proper clothing, boots, etc. and follow the lessons of precaution of where we walk, place our hands and explore."

The group nodded their heads, as they have been through the Jr. Park Ranger lessons teaching them about safety from snakes.

"Finally, number 10," Warren announced in excitement. "Number 10 is the timber rattler."

"Yikes," said Jack, jokingly. "Yes, and opposite the copperhead these snakes are more above the 3,000 foot level."

"Thanks, Jack and Warren, that is a great list. Before we move on, are there any questions?" Brock asked.

A few of the Jr. Park Rangers raised their hands. Brock would point to one at a time.

"What about elk, aren't they dangerous?" Gunner, one of the Jr. Park Rangers asked.

"Yes, Gunner," Brock replied. "Elk are the largest animals in the park, weighing up to 900 pounds. The rules are to stay 50 feet or more away from an elk. An elk will charge if felt threatened, and with his body mass and horns they can do some damage. Mating season is a sensitive time, but also when they are feeding too."

Brock then pointed at another Jr. Park Ranger who had a question.

"What about raccoons?" Mason asked.

"Certainly, raccoons are dangerous too," Brock answered Mason. "Raccoons have sharp claws and teeth, but like many animals, can carry diseases like rabies. Listen, we all know that many animals can cause death. But each of you have learned through your lessons on how to respect nature and animals in their natural habitat. Show that respect and teach others to do the same. This is what will keep the animals and everyone safe."

"Yes," said Jack. "If you approach an animal so closely that it changes its behavior, you have become too close."

"Exactly!" stated Brock. "Let's all give Warren and Jack a big hand on the list."

The group applauded as they appreciated the information. Most Jr. Park Rangers simply enjoy learning, and part of that learning is hearing it in different ways.

"Okay, let's move forward," Brock stated.

The group hiked for about an hour more, enjoying the views of the trail. The hike itself was enjoyable. The important aspect to Brock and Bronson was that the hike was a learning experience. The Great Smoky Mountains National Park is too large to show them everything, every tree, plant and creature. But that is not the point of the hike. The point of the hike is to let the Jr. Park Rangers enjoy part of the park, and to learn about the specifics of this park. In addition, the more they learn the more they fall in love with preserving all parks. This is a lesson not only for the youth, but for adults as well. Soon the group made it back to the bus. They made sure everyone was accounted for and then proceeded back to the Sugarland Visitors Center.

As they arrived back to the Sugarland Visitors Center they could see that other groups were arriving back too. Everyone was orderly, but you could tell there was excitement on what each group did for their event and what was learned. The Jr. Park Rangers were ushered back to the presentation room where there were refreshments for them to enjoy. Jack and Warren mingled with some of the other groups, but soon the meeting was going to start. Ranger Johnson entered and walked to the front of the room.

"Okay everyone, let's get started," Ranger Johnson announced. He allowed the volume in the room to settle down as the Jr. Park Rangers grabbed their seats. He appreciated how respectful they were in giving their attention. "Now, did we have all a good time with our groups?!" he asked enthusiastically.

"Yes, sir!" was the loud reply back from the Jr. Park Ranger group.

"Awesome," he stated. "Well, let's get started. I am going to call the group leaders of each group to come and talk about their trip, what they observed and what they learned. I will monitor the time as you each will have 15-minutes which will allow for orderly questions from the audience." Ranger Johnson then called on group number one to start. The groups each presented one by one. There was excitement in the presenters' voice and answers to questions. You could see and feel their enthusiasm as well as the audience's excitement. The Jr. Park Rangers were always very respectful. But they truly wanted to hear what each group did. There is always so much to do and learn in each State and National Park, and by hearing what others did, allowed them to experience it as well. Many of the Jr. Park Rangers share the stories with their families and it helps when they return on a family trip to have a good sense of what they want to experience. Each group presented and the event was near its completion. Jack and Warren had not heard from Brock what they would be doing that evening. Park Ranger Johnson then made an announcement to the group, "Okay, let's give all the presenters a round of applause."

The group applauded for each other.

"Great!" Ranger Johnson exclaimed. "Now we have some exciting news for you. From here, we will stay in our groups and our buses will take us near the Elkmont Campground. We are taking you to see the awesome Synchronous Elkmont Firefly Event here in the Great Smoky Mountains!"

The group jumped to their feet with a loud roar and applause. Most of the Jr. Park Rangers knew about the Synchronous Elkmont Firefly Event as it is well-known and a special feature of the Great Smoky Mountains. Jack and Warren were as excited as everyone else, and Brock was excited for them. The groups gathered together and reloaded their buses. They were all enthusiastic, although a little tired from the hike of the day. The buses were loaded. Brock and Bronson made sure everyone was accounted for and they departed. The bus was a little quieter for this trip. The ride was uneventful and was relatively short, so soon they arrived. They exited the bus in an orderly fashion and upon arrival were met with burgers and hot dogs, which was an awesome treat as each one of them were hungry. Soon it was time to view and attend the event.

THE SYNCHRONOUS FIREFLY EVENT

The Synchronous Firefly Event is only available for about two weeks each year, in late May or early June, so it was a great surprise to the group and perfect timing. Synchronous fireflies are one of at least 19 species of fireflies that live in the Great Smoky Mountains National Park. They are the only species in America whose individuals can synchronize their flashing light patterns. The fireflies are actually beetles. Their light patterns are part of their mating display. The distinct flashing pattern of the synchronous fireflies is difficult to describe and nearly impossible to photograph or catch on film. The pattern includes five to eight bursts of light in a short time period followed by complete darkness for approximately five seconds. The light they emit, which produces no heat, is due to a chemical reaction of luciferin and oxygen and is used to attract a mate.

The Jr. Park Rangers had blankets to sit on. Brock and his fellow Park Rangers had folding chairs. Everyone was excited for the event. As the evening darkened, it soon started. The males are the ones that are flying around, as the females stay close to the ground. The males flash as a pattern and when a female becomes interested she flashes from the ground. No one is sure why the fireflies flash synchronously. Competition between males may be one reason: they all want to be the first to flash. Or perhaps if the males all flash together they have a better chance of being noticed, and the females can make better comparisons. It was a beautiful sight, to see how they synchronize, but also how they light up against the dark sky. This was a treat for the group as other observers have to participate in a lottery to win an opportunity to attend. This appeared to be the peak part of the two week appearance, which means at that time the greatest number of the fireflies are displaying. The event lasted for some time, several hours to be exact, and it had been a long and satisfying day for the group. Soon they all gathered up their blankets, and of course any trash, and by group they hiked back to their buses. Each bus verified their groups before leaving. Jack and Warren exchanged emails and phone numbers with Jr. Park Rangers from other groups they met. They were always a little sad when their meetings were done, but always happy with making new friends.

On the bus, Jack and Warren talked about the beauty of the Synchronous Firefly Event and how blessed they were to be able to see it. The Jr. Park Ranger motto of pay it forward always miraculously seems to come back in unexpected blessings. Jack became deep in thought. When the wildfire

Synchronous Elkmont Fireflies

was occurring in 2016 he would keep up on the news, but having the ability to come and see the Great Smoky Mountains was a true blessing as well. Brock was going to take him and Warren to several places to show how close the fire came to certain areas and hotels, especially in Gatlinburg. He had promised them other places as there is so much to see. Jack had read about Cherokee on the North Carolina's side, Clingmans Dome, and all the fun attractions of Pigeon

Forge. Warren desired to see the observation tower built at Clingmans Dome. The tower, built in 1959 and listed on the National Register of Historic Places, offers a panoramic view of the Great Smoky Mountains. An air quality monitoring station, operated by the Environmental Protection Agency, is the second highest in eastern North America. Like so many things that are great, the Great Smoky Mountains National Park and its surrounding areas has just too many features to see on one visit. Jack and Warren could not wait to come back with their sister and parents. After all, their sister is next in line in joining the Jr. Park Ranger Program and it is important to educate the adults too. Jack and Warren were thankful to be led by Park Ranger Brock. He certainly is a leader and a legend to learn from.

THE END

Made in the USA
Monee, IL
16 September 2022

14105822R00038